MW00654828

Mindfucking

Being surrounded by bullshit is one thing. Having your mind fucked is quite another. The former is irritating, but the latter is violating and intrusive (unless you give your consent). If someone manipulates your thoughts and emotions, messing with your head, you naturally feel resentment: he or she has distorted your perceptions, disturbed your feelings, maybe even usurped your self. Mindfucking is a prevalent aspect of contemporary culture and the agent can range from an individual to a whole state, from personal mind games to wholesale propaganda. In *Mindfucking* Colin McGinn investigates and clarifies this phenomenon. Taking in the ancient Greeks, Shakespeare and modern techniques of thought control, McGinn assembles the conceptual components of this most complex of concepts – trust, deception, emotion, manipulation, false belief, vulnerability – and explores its very nature. He elucidates the sexual implications of the metaphor of mindfucking, stressing both its positive and negative features and exposes its essence of psychological upheaval and disorientation. Delusion is the general result, sometimes insanity. How mindfucked are you? It's hard to say from the inside, but being aware of the phenomenon offers at least some protection.

Mindfucking

Mindfucking
A Critique of Mental Manipulation

❧

Colin McGinn

ACUMEN

First published in 2008 by Acumen
Reprinted 2008

Acumen Publishing Limited
Stocksfield Hall
Stocksfield
NE43 7TN
www.acumenpublishing.co.uk

ISBN: 978-1-84465-114-6 (hardcover)

British Library Cataloguing-in-Publication Data
A catalogue record for this book is available
from the British Library.

Designed and typeset by Kate Williams, Swansea.
Printed and bound by Cromwell Press, Trowbridge, Wiltshire

The Moor is of a free and open nature,
That thinks men honest that but seem to be so,
And will as tenderly be led by th' nose,
As asses are.

(Iago, in Othello, Act 1 Scene 3)

❧ Contents

❧ Preface

It was Harry Frankfurt's groundbreaking discussion of bullshit, in the aptly named *On Bullshit*, that prompted me to undertake a similar enquiry into a related (but distinct) concept: the concept of *mindfucking*. These are both concepts in wide circulation, but their meanings have not been systematically articulated, for a number of reasons. And they are concepts of some intellectual and cultural significance, not to be confused with other allied concepts. Just as Frankfurt argues, convincingly, that bullshitting is not the same thing as lying, so, I shall contend, mindfucking is not the same thing as bullshitting, although all three concepts belong together, in that each implies some sort of abuse of the truth (of what kind is one of

the main questions to be answered). The concept
of the mindfuck is of more recent vintage than
that of bullshit – certainly the word itself is newer
– and is still, perhaps, in the process of establish-
ing itself, so that my enquiry might well be seen as
consolidating a concept as yet in its infancy. But,
like bullshit, mindfucking is a prevalent aspect of
contemporary culture, and we do well to attempt
an articulate understanding of it. Just as we have all
been bullshitted to (bullshat?) at one time or another,
so we have probably also suffered our share of mindfucking – and it cannot hurt to understand what has
thereby been perpetrated on us. It is always excellent
advice to know one's enemy.

   I first came across the word "mindfuck" about
fifteen years ago. I had given a public lecture in New
York, on the mind–body problem and consciousness, in which I advanced a radical thesis designed
to shake up the complacency of my audience in

respect of this most vexing of subjects, and a friend
reported to me that a student of his had referred to
my presentation as a "mindfuck". I knew instantly
what was meant, although the expression was new
to me: I knew the nature of my argument in the
lecture, and I could put together my lexical grasp of
the words "mind" and "fuck" in such a way as to
appreciate what features of my presentation were
being alluded to in this striking locution. The expression stayed with me (I was, we might say, mildly
mindfucked by the word "mindfuck") and I began
to notice other uses of it, usually more negative
in character. But it was not until I read Frankfurt's
free-ranging *On Bullshit* that I had any idea of
investigating the concept more thoroughly and
systematically. It now seems to me a concept with
a future (the word "bullshit", although still widely
used, of course, has a ring of 1950s America to me):
the mindfuck is something we shall hear a lot more

about. I doubt if anyone knows who coined the term (just as who came up with the word "bullshit" is now lost in the mists of time), but, whoever it was, he or she was on to something. There is a phenomenon of human life here that cries out for a pungent name of its own, along with an associated analysis.

Preliminary delineation of the concept

Not everyone is perhaps familiar with the vernacular term "mindfuck", although the constituent words themselves are suggestive of at least some of its sense as a composite expression. The term brings together a pair of incongruous elements – one mental, the other physical – to produce a kind of internal semantic dissonance (lexical friction, we might say). It feels oxymoronic, yet intelligible. Hearing the expression, we naturally form the idea of some sort of assault on the mind, an invasive operation performed on the psychological state of the person. The sexual meaning of "fuck" suggests something unusually intimate, and potentially violating, even violent, although a connotation of the pleasurable is not ruled out. But it is a type of fucking directed towards the mental part of a person, not the bodily part (not that regular fucking has no mental target). The online encyclopedia Wikipedia has defined it succinctly thus: "*Mindfuck* means either a thing that messes with the minds of those exposed to it or the act of doing so". The HarperCollins *American Slang* has the following entry under "mind-fuck" (they retain the hyphen): "To manipulate someone to think and act as one wishes", and it equates the word with "brain-wash". The *Oxford English Dictionary* (*OED*) offers a greater variety of definitions. As a noun, the word is defined as "An imaginary act of sexual intercourse" and "A disturbing or revelatory experience, esp. one which is drug-induced or is caused by deliberate psychological manipulation. Also: deception". As a verb, we have "To manipulate or otherwise interfere with a person's psyche; to disturb psychologically". The *OED* dates the first uses of the term to the

1960s, when drugs and political manipulation were salient cultural features, citing such uses as: "Their consciousness has been permanently altered. Forever altered. They've been mind-fucked", and "He rarely gets a hard-on, but the mind-fuck is really irresistible" (said of a Hollywood big-shot). These are perfectly adequate definitions, providing clear directions for how the term is to be employed, but they are only a beginning to enquiry. We need to be much more precise about the notion of "messing" with someone's mind or manipulating a person's psyche, and about the scope and limits of the concept. What exactly is involved in manipulating a person's mind in this particular way? How widely does the concept apply? Is being mindfucked a good or a bad thing?

To physically fuck someone is undoubtedly to "mess" with them in some way, and bodily "manipulation" is clearly implicated. To mindfuck someone, by analogy, is to mess with that person's mind in a comparable fashion: it is some sort of interference or intervention or invasion. It is an action with a result and an associated means. We should distinguish the *act* of mindfucking from the *vehicle* of it. The former use – "mindfuck" as a verb – is perhaps more natural than the latter – "mindfuck" as a noun denoting some type of entity – but both uses are legitimate and useful. Thus one may refer to a particular piece of discourse or a film as a mindfuck, as well as to the process of mindfucking somebody by performing suitable acts. In both cases we are speaking of something done to the mind that bears some resemblance to what is done to the body (and whole person) when that person is penetrated sexually: either the process or its vehicle. The question is what exactly this resemblance is supposed to consist in (it is certainly not a matter of literally inserting a phallic object into the brain!). Where precisely does the analogy lie?

We should note, to begin with, that the meaning of "mindfuck" is not exclusively negative. When my lecture on the mind–body problem was described in that way, the intent was not negative: I was said to be messing with people's minds in some fashion, but the suggestion was not that this was illegitimate or morally objectionable. Also, the phrase is sometimes used to describe the positive sensation involved in having, or being presented with, some striking new idea, or having some sort of agreeably life-altering experience (hence the *OED*'s mention of a "revelatory" experience). Indeed, in some uses of the word, mindfucking is what happens in a certain kind of romantic encounter, when the other person somehow operates pleasurably on the mind to produce a welcome reaction (we shall consider later whether all romantic love is a species of mindfucking.) When a book or film or conversation is described as a mindfuck, this can be taken as a favourable evaluation: the psychological messing that has occurred is of the desirable kind. Perhaps there is always a tinge of danger in such a mindfuck, but the result is nonetheless regarded positively. This makes the word "mindfuck" different from "bullshit" and "lie": there is no *good* kind of bullshitting or lying, to be set beside the bad kinds. There may be white lies and harmless bullshit (as in the "bull sessions" so well described by Frankfurt), but this is not to say that such things are positively excellent; they are intrinsically bad things whose natural badness has been neutralized or bracketed. You cannot imagine a correct use of "bullshit" or "liar" to compliment somebody ("Hey, that was a great piece of bullshit you gave us today", or "That was one of the most commendable lies I've ever fallen for"), except ironically. But you can use "mindfuck" in a fully complimentary sense, as when you enthusiastically assert, "Go to see *Fight Club*, it's a terrific

mindfuck". We cannot sort lies and bullshit into
two piles – the good examples and the bad ones
– but mindfucks do seem to come in two distinct
varieties. I may go to the cinema or to a lecture *hoping*
for a mindfuck, but I cannot in this way (except
masochistically) hope to be lied to or bullshitted to.
Of course, this duality in the sense of "mindfuck"
reflects its origins in describing the act of sexual
intercourse, since there are also two kinds of that
activity too: the good kind and the not so good kind.
That is, there is the welcomed act of intercourse
and there is the imposed act: the act of voluntary
intercourse and the act of rape (as well as the reluctant but voluntary kind, and no doubt others).
Mindfucking, like ordinary fucking, is not *by definition*
bad or undesirable, although it certainly may be.
But the concepts of lying and bullshitting are more
like the concept of rape: these are all bad things by
definition.

However, that said, I think that the common use of "mindfuck" is *generally* negative. This is the predominant sense of the word: what it usually connotes. We generally resent being mindfucked, blaming those responsible; and the techniques of mindfucking (which we need to investigate) are generally deployed to nefarious ends. It is this negative understanding of the term that I shall be primarily concerned with in what follows, although the positive use will also continue to be relevant. The definition in terms of "messing with the mind" conveys this negative connotation, since messing with someone is not something done in the best interests of that person, and a mess is not something we favour. To mess with someone is to leave them *in* a mess. Mindfucking is, we might say, *prima facie* a bad thing, although in certain circumstances this badness can be overridden or reversed or channelled towards something desirable. So the concept does not behave

exactly like its model – physical fucking – since there
is no presumption of negativity in the use of *that*
concept. Put differently, "mindfuck" is closer in its
meaning to "rape" than the simple "fuck" is, despite
its potential for favourable use in certain special
cases. I would not be surprised if the term originated
as wholly negative in meaning and then acquired
a subsidiary use in the favourable sense (perhaps
like the word "bang" used to describe sexual intercourse). In any case, I shall be primarily concerned
with its negative employment in what follows: the
kind of mindfucking it is proper to resent.

There are some related locutions that help to
clarify the meaning of our term, and also attest to
its presumption of negativity. The closest is perhaps
"fuck with a person's head". We have that occur-
rence of "fuck" again, only now with "head" used as
an idiomatic variant of "mind", although it carries a
more corporeal connotation, and no doubt suggests

fellatio. Fellatio simply is a kind of head fucking ("giving/getting head"), and to fuck *with* someone's head is to effect this kind of action on it. If you have successfully fucked with someone's head, then you have surely mindfucked that person; this is, as philosophers say, analytic (a tautology). To speak of fucking with someone's head is to focus more on the process than the result, but a successful act of this kind is aptly described as a case of mindfucking: it has the state of being mindfucked as its result. To accuse someone of trying to fuck with your head *is* to accuse them of trying to mindfuck you. In this linguistic vicinity, we also have the phrases "playing mind games" and "pushing your buttons". In these locutions, the most instructive elements relate to the notion of a game and to that of sensitive points of the psyche that can be activated. The notion of a game suggests that the perpetrator's intentions are not serious, in the sense that that person is seriously concerned to convey the truth or to elicit emotions appropriate to the actual situation. Sincerely informing someone of the facts is not a "mind *game*", although it aims to induce a psychological result, namely belief or knowledge. To be a mind game proper an action (or series of actions) has to be a kind of pretence: something phoney or fake or dishonest (I shall come back to this in the next section). The idea of sensitive psychic buttons brings in the realm of emotional receptivity: exploiting such sensitivity to achieve a particular end (generally a morally dubious one). To push someone's buttons is to *exploit* them emotionally: to use their emotions against them. It falls into the category of *abuse*. Putting these various expressions together, then, we may speak of fucking with somebody's head by playing mind games on them, pushing their buttons and, as a result, mindfucking the individual in question. To put it in less slangy terms, one may interfere with a person's psychological equilibrium by playing on their emotional sensitivities, and leaving that person in a state of mental violation. The more pungent language contained in the street vernacular version suggests the aggressive and ruthless nature of the act, and the devastation that can result. The vigour of the words suggests the intensity of the act and its psychological consequences.

It is notable (and perhaps regrettable) that there exists no respectable term for the phenomenon in question, and little in the way of euphemism. In this, "mindfuck" resembles "bullshit". As Frankfurt observes, we do have words like "humbug", "balder-dash" and "hot air", but none of these quite adds up to "bullshit", which suggests something quite specific and pernicious. Since the term is so descriptively useful, it has developed euphemistic contractions, such as "bull" or "BS", so that the concept can be invoked in a wider variety of social situations. The word "mindfuck" also lacks a respectable synonym; so it is not merely slang for something we have already named and classified (although, as we shall see later, certain sub-varieties of it have their own respectable terms). Nor, I think, is there anything in the language that does the job of "humbug" in relation to "bullshit": no watering down of the concept. The closest we get is the substitution of "mess" for "fuck", but this leads us to the feeble "mind-mess": it does not convey the right idea at all. The intended concept is expressed by no other term of the language, as far as I can see, so we are compelled to stick with the vulgar expression. We do not even have an established contraction of the word to take the sting out of it, as with "BS" for "bullshit" and "mofo" for "motherfucker". No one now speaks of "MFing" somebody, although that would be a feasible substitute, and "mind-hump" has no currency on the street.

(I recently came across a new television show called "Mindfreak", a thinly disguised variant on "mindfuck", but "mindfreak" is linguistically limited as an overall stand-in.) We must, accordingly, stick with the austere purity of "mindfuck" and make the best of it. The more you say it the less offensive it sounds; to me, now, it is a technical term, more or less drained of shock-value.

I trust that we now have an adequate basic understanding of the term. We can then go on to use it to describe particular situations, products and processes. This should help to elucidate further the import of the concept. It may sound strange for me to say this, but I think the origins of the concept of the mindfuck go back at least as far as Plato (so this essay is yet another footnote to Plato). For Plato was strenuously concerned to combat those orators of ancient Greece known as the Sophists, in effect, the earliest mindfuckers we have on record.

The Sophists undertook, for a fee, to win any argument, especially in a court of law, by any means they could muster. Their aim was not to argue for the truth, using only valid arguments and true premises; they felt free to win assent by any means possible, using rhetorical tricks, attractive fallacies, appeals to sympathetic emotion, fear, prejudice and all the rest. Instead of employing only the means of rational persuasion, engaging with the audience's faculty of reason, they resorted to methods of psychological manipulation. They cajoled and seduced, messing with the minds of their audience, and had no compunction about the use of fallacies and falsehoods. Moreover, they would teach you how to do this too: to become a fucker of minds yourself. The essence of their technique was to persuade not by appealing to the rational faculties but by tapping into emotion (sound familiar?). Plato was deeply opposed to the Sophists, valuing rational discourse as he did, and he was keen to distinguish sharply between the rational procedures of genuine philosophers like himself and the bag of psychological tricks deployed by the Sophists.

From this historical example we can see that mindfucking is to be contrasted, first and foremost, with rational persuasion: it is a type of rhetorical abuse or sleight-of-hand. It is essentially deceptive or dishonest (in its negative connotation). By definition, then, there can be no such thing as a rational mindfuck (in the negative sense); the mindfuck is manipulative, not rationally persuasive. This is important; you cannot be accused of culpably mindfucking someone by presenting a *good argument*, although there may be cases in which convincing someone of something by rational means is the morally wrong thing to do (say, convincing a child that its parents are in mortal danger when no particular purpose is served by this, even though it is true). A person may resent being persuaded of something by rational means, but they cannot rightly protest that they have been mindfucked. Of course, the Sophists *purported* to be using rational persuasion (how could they not, if they intended to persuade?), but in reality they were pushing buttons and fucking with heads. They were early and expert practitioners of the "art of the mindfuck".

A more benign example of mindfucking can be seen at work in Thomas Kuhn's well-known notion of a "paradigm shift" in *The Structure of Scientific Revolutions*. This is an example of the positive sense of the term, since paradigm shifts are generally in the direction of truth (or at least greater theoretical adequacy). The reason I bring this notion into the discussion is that paradigm shifts involve a deep shift in viewpoint, a radical re-orientation of thought. They inspire shock and awe, and they are felt as profoundly disturbing, if also exhilarating.

Thus, when the geocentric theory of the universe
was replaced with the heliocentric theory, people had
their entire perspective on the universe thoroughly
overhauled, with deep consequences for the place
of man in the scheme of things. This must have
felt profoundly disturbing, as if everything you
have believed has just been demolished and you
must begin to live in a new intellectual world. In
other words, the shift of paradigm felt like a mindfuck: a far-reaching conceptual upheaval. We are
not the centre of the universe! Similarly, in the
case of Darwin's revolution. Digesting Darwin was
certainly a mind-altering experience, an upheaval of
thought; no wonder many people still cannot wrap
their heads around it. A change of paradigm, as
Kuhn conceives it, is a fundamental restructuring of
outlook, often with deep emotional resonance, and
frequently coupled with resistance, and this seems
aptly characterized as a mindfuck (of the benign

variety, although it can be experienced as painful and be effected only reluctantly). It is no casual replacement of one belief by another, but a seismic shift in worldview. Thus we tend to speak in such cases of a revolution in "consciousness", not merely in beliefs. (The change might be compared to losing one's virginity, when a whole new world opens up.) In a paradigm shift there is strong initial resistance, which is finally overcome, and the recipients of the new perspective enter a new phase of consciousness: a new reality. Whenever science subverts a central and entrenched tenet of common sense, we have a case of mindfucking (although in the positive sense, since science is a form of rational enquiry). Learning the extent and nature of the physical universe, with those enormous magnitudes and impossible quantities, is a kind of mindfuck, in that it disturbs ordinary complacent assumptions about the world we live in. The bizarre world of quantum theory is likewise one of the biggest scientific mindfucks to date. And Einstein's relativity theory is a mindfuck on our views of space and time. These revolutions in scientific understanding have the capacity to stagger and disturb; they do more than merely replace one belief with another. This psychological fact about the scientific enterprise seems to me worth recording and highlighting; certainly, it is not the emotionally neutral accumulation of data.

I said that the mindfuck (in the negative sense) is to be contrasted with rational argument, with the Sophists on one side and Plato on the other. But according to some recent theorists – often known as "postmodernists" – this contrast is itself delusory, a kind of sophistry. For them, *all* discourse is an exercise of rhetorical (and other) power, with nothing counting as objective, rational persuasion. Truth, in particular, is not the proper aim of intellectual enquiry (the philosopher Richard Rorty talks

this way). Any discourse purporting to be more
than the mere expression of subjectivity or solidar-
ity is itself a mindfuck, and the biggest one of all,
promoting the delusion that there is such a thing as
objective truth. For the card-carrying postmodernist, our standard institutions of discourse, at least
as they have been historically understood – science,
history, philosophy and so on – are all at bottom
guilty of mindfucking, since they all subscribe to
the spurious ideal of objective truth and rational
argument. The only thing to do is to unmask the
delusion and acknowledge that there is nothing but
subjectivity and community; we must expose the
mindfuck for what it is. Now, it is not that I have any
sympathy with this point of view, which I think is
easily refuted (but that is not my job here); I mention
it now only to illustrate how the concept of mindfucking connects with more familiar types of view.
The postmodernist believes, in effect, that we have

all been brainwashed into accepting the idea of universal reason and objective reality, but that this is just a giant mindfuck, powered by capitalism, patriarchy or what have you. We must be liberated from the effects of this mindfuck by revealing it for what it is: brute psychological manipulation with an ulterior motive. So the *concept* is at work in this kind of position, even if it is not called by the name we are here considering. For the postmodernist, psychological manipulation is dressing itself up as rational argument (an outmoded concept). Plato, from this perspective, is a Sophist in disguise, precisely because he subscribes to the spurious ideals of truth, reason and objective reality, the great Platonic mindfuck of Western civilization.

Can a mindfuck, in the sense I have sketchily delineated so far, lead to any consequences analogous to the kind regularly produced by physical intercourse? The question is not as frivolous as it may sound; we need to know how far the metaphor extends, and hence how deep it goes. So, is there an analogue of pregnancy, and progeny? I think there is; a mindfuck can plant seeds in the mind that cause it to conceive a new life, and that life may go forth into the world and multiply. This is clearly true of the kind of benign mindfuck that goes with a paradigm shift, since the new viewpoint will take root in the mind, grow, reach maturity, and be expelled into the world, where it will work to impregnate the minds of others. We have here an analogue of biological reproduction. Richard Dawkins, in *The Selfish Gene*, introduced the idea of the *meme* by analogy with the gene; just as alien genes are introduced into the mother by the father, and then passed on to the offspring, so memes are communicated from one mind to another, and then propagate themselves in the minds of multiple others. The reproduction of memes (items of information) is thus compared by Dawkins to the reproduction of genes, as if the transmission of ideas were a kind of mental sex, and what is this but the idea of the mindfuck? The mindfuck involves planting seeds in someone else's mind that then take on a life of their own and may spread through the population. And there are two types of memes to contend with: the good ones and the bad ones. The good ones are like new paradigms that proceed from a sound, rational basis; they pass from person to person by rational persuasion (Plato approved of this kind of meme). But there are also the malign kinds that simply get their hooks into people's minds and will not let go; this is the negative mindfuck. Dawkins gives the example of jingles: the tune gets into your head, takes up residence and will not let you go – you have been musically mind-fucked. The jingle-writer knows your brain has a weakness for catchy tunes and silly rhymes and plays on this to get the advertising jingles into your head, which you may then go around humming, passing the meme on to others. You have been mentally interfered with, cranially molested. The same is true of catchphrases, clichés and prejudices; these are all cases of being mindfucked, negatively so. They are memes that spread through different people's minds by a process analogous to impregnation. The meme is to mindfucking what the gene is to the regular kind. And just as we have to be careful who we have sex with, given the consequences for pregnancy and reproduction (not to mention disease), so we have to be careful about the mindfucking that goes on around us; we do not want those pesky memes in our head, messing us up, polluting the mental land-scape. In any event, the metaphor of mindfucking has its corollaries in the notion of mental impregna-tion and reproduction; it does not stop at the simple act. The locution is doubly apt. Sometimes the act of mindfucking has no such consequence – it is just a passing episode, leaving no permanent mark – but there are times when something is left in the mind to grow and mutate, and burgeon forth into the world. This idea of potential permanence is also part of the intent of the metaphor; you may end up mind*fucked* for life.

❧ Deeper into mindfucking

In the previous section we became accustomed to the term and how it can be used; now we must analyse the phenomenon to which it refers more carefully. We want to know the *nature* of the mindfuck, what its constituent components are. I suggest it belongs to the same family of concepts as lying and bullshitting, which is not to say that they are identical, but that they resemble each other in significant respects. Our first task, then, is to locate the concept of mindfucking in relation to these other concepts: how is it similar and how is it different? (I shall here be considering the negative kind.) The chief respect in which they resemble each other is that they all involve deception in some way, or at the very least lack of transparency; they are not *honest*.

The value that guides them is not truthfulness, or the desire to achieve truth. The lie is the easiest of the three to understand; its deception is the most straightforward. It deceives about two things: how the world objectively stands, and how things stand in the liar's own mind. If I tell you a lie to the effect that your spouse is unfaithful, I mislead you about two matters: the state of fidelity of your spouse, and what I believe about this matter. I lead you to believe that things are other than they really are in the world, and I lead you to believe that my own beliefs are other than they are. I thus flatly contradict the truth in two ways: I state the opposite of the truth about both the world and my beliefs about it. My intention in lying can therefore be characterized as a deliberate flouting of the truth in these two domains. If the lie succeeds, you will be wrong about the world *and* about me; I will have infected you with error at two points.

But, as Frankfurt argues, the bullshitter does not in this direct way flout the truth; his relation to the truth is more complex and subtle. For him, truth and falsehood are *optional* properties of a statement. The truth-teller must go for truth, and the liar must go for falsehood; but the bullshitter can go either way, depending on what suits him. He is *indifferent* to the truth (and to the false). Frankfurt writes:

Someone who lies and someone who tells the truth are playing on opposite sides, so to speak, in the same game. Each responds to the facts as he understands them, although the response of the one is guided by the authority of truth, while the response of the other defies that authority and refuses to meet its demands. The bullshitter ignores these demands altogether. He does not reject the authority of truth, as the liar does, and oppose himself to it. He pays no attention

to it at all. By virtue of this, bullshit is a greater
enemy of the truth than lies are.*

The bullshitter is depicted here as uninterested in the
truth even when he knows it; truth and falsehood
are simply not part of the language game (to use
Wittgenstein's term) he is engaged in. The bullshitter aims neither at truth nor at falsehood; he stands
magnificently aloof from such concerns.

One sees what Frankfurt is driving at in this
analysis of bullshit, but as it stands it is inadequate,
for a person could be engaging in speech acts in
sublime indifference to the truth without thereby
bullshitting; he might simply be telling a fictional
story or practising elocution. In these linguistic activities, the speaker is attempting neither to
tell the truth nor to lie, but he is not bullshitting

---

* Harry G. Frankfurt, *On Bullshit* (Princeton, NJ: Princeton University
  Press, 2005), 60–61.

anybody. What is missing – and perhaps Frankfurt
took this to be understood – is that he is *purporting
to tell the truth* while actually not caring either way.
He is endeavouring to give his listener the impression that he is aiming at the truth, when actually
he could not care less; he merely wants to give an
impression of truthfulness, without really living up to
that impression. In a standard case, he is trying to
produce the impression that he knows what he is
talking about when in reality he does not, and says
whatever he thinks will aid that impression. He is, as
Frankfurt elsewhere says, *bluffing*: trying to hoodwink
his audience. He does not want to be caught out in
a falsehood, but falsehood will serve him as well as
truth so long as it produces the impression he seeks
to promote. He is indifferent about the very thing he
is purporting to care about.

According to the way I am putting the point, as
opposed to Frankfurt's way, the bullshitter is actually

similar to the liar in one central respect: he is trying
to produce a false belief in his listener, namely
the belief that the impression he seeks to give of
himself is the correct impression. Thus he is aiming
to produce a false belief in his listener; he is *not*
indifferent about *this* question of truth. The liar aims
at a double deception: about the way the world is
and about what his state of belief is. The bullshitter
keeps one half of this deception, since he too wishes
to produce a false belief about himself: generally,
that he knows what he is talking about. So the
bullshitter is not as far from the liar as Frankfurt's
analysis suggests; he *is* intentionally misrepresent-
ing himself – as competent, sincere, concerned and
so on. But I do not want to quibble with the details
of Frankfurt's analysis of bullshit; my eye is on the
logical structure of the mindfuck. And the crucial
point of difference between lying and bullshitting,
on the one hand, and mindfucking, on the other, is

that the former two are concerned exclusively with the beliefs of the listener, while the mindfucker is concerned with the listener's beliefs *and emotions*. The liar and the bullshitter aim to produce a cognitive effect – namely, false belief – while the mindfucker has a wider aim: to affect the emotional state of the victim. The mindfucker is not satisfied if he can make you *think* certain things that are not true; he wants you to *feel* a certain way – characteristically, a bad way. Hence the reference in the dictionary definitions to the production of a *disturbing* effect in the listener. The mindfucker aims at the psyche as a whole, while the liar and the bullshitter are content to focus on the belief component of the psyche.

What are the emotions that a mindfuck seeks to arouse? They are no doubt of many kinds, but the following are characteristic: alarm, confusion, dismay, jealousy, anger, misery, insecurity, fear and hatred. In extreme cases, the desired emotional effect might be total personal disintegration (we shall look at some examples in the next section). This goes far beyond what the liar and bullshitter aim for; the mindfucker has a far more ambitious agenda. The production of these emotions might serve a further end, of course, notably to manipulate the victim into behaving in a certain way that suits the purposes of the perpetrator. But the emotional interference is the essential mechanism of the project. This concern is signalled in the term itself, since fucking has far greater emotional resonance than mere excreting (we find shit repugnant, but it does not disturb our emotional core). The mindfucker must accordingly be something of a psychologist. He must know how to manipulate the emotions of others, and in such a way that his true intentions are kept hidden. It helps, if you are going to be a successful mindfucker, to have psychological insight, particularly about the idiosyncrasies of your victims (it must be a particular temptation for psychoanalysts and the like). The skilled liar must be able to present a convincing case for what is false, and similarly for the bullshitter; but the mindfucker must be skilled at manipulating the psychology of the victim, which is another kind of skill altogether. A consummate liar or bullshitter might therefore not be a very good mindfucker (although the reverse is unlikely to be true, since mindfucking involves deception too). Mindfucking therefore presents a greater challenge, since it brings in more psychological machinery; it requires another kind of intelligence.

Emotions enter at two points in the mindfucking project: as a means and as an end. As an end, the purpose is to produce a state of emotional disturbance (and this may serve a further end); as a means, the first thing is achieved by playing on the emotional vulnerabilities of the victim. Since a part of the project will be to produce false beliefs in the victim, this means that these beliefs will be produced by applying pressure to the victim's emotions: pushing their buttons. The mindfucker will typically play on the anxieties and insecurities of the victim in order to produce a set of false beliefs, which will then lead to the emotional disturbance that is sought as an end. The most obvious example involves jealousy: the mindfucker wants to persuade you that your beloved is unfaithful and does so by working on your insecurities, as a result of which you experience the disturbing emotion of jealousy. Of course, someone might be trying to bullshit you and mindfuck you at the same time, in which case they will employ just these emotional means; but the point I am making is that it is not *intrinsic* to bullshitting that it aims at psychological disturbance of an emotional kind, whereas this *is* intrinsic to mindfucking. It would be quite mistaken, therefore, to think that mindfucking is just an extreme kind of bullshitting, as mistaken as supposing that bullshitting is just extreme lying. These concepts are all distinct from each other, despite belonging to the same family.

What are the weaknesses that are exploited? Again, they can be of many kinds, but the most effective pertain to irrational fears. Irrational fears, by definition, do not require a cogent case to be made for them to rise up, so they are particularly useful to the dedicated mindfucker. The fear of being attacked or usurped is a potent one to exploit; insecurities about physical appearance can offer fertile ground; vague anxieties about the future are also readily tapped into. Phobias are the easiest of all, since they are irrational in their very nature and are easily evoked. I once met a woman with a serious phobia of butterflies, even dead ones pinned under glass; it would have been child's play to mindfuck her by hinting at the presence of butterflies under the bed. The mindfucker is a student of human weakness and vulnerability, using these traits to create false beliefs and emotional chaos. Perhaps this is part of the reason the mindfucker seems a more unsavoury character than the bullshitter (for whom we reserve a modicum of pity). The mindfuck (in the negative sense) is a dark and sinister thing, going far beyond the merely cognitive wrongdoing of the kind perpetrated by lies and bullshit.

I have lately been focusing on the *result* end of the mindfuck: the effect it seeks to bring about. Now I must say something about the act itself: the kind of agency it involves. This will round out our picture of the concept. The prime point here is that it involves the illegitimate exercise of power. The victim of the mindfuck is exploited, leaned on, invaded, imposed on, controlled and manipulated. Mindfucking is an inherently aggressive act. It is an act of psychological violence, more or less extreme. As such, it is clearly immoral. The intention behind it is morally

objectionable: it is an intention to do harm. This is
clearly the implied meaning of the term; the idea
of domination is built into the concept. That is not
to say it can never be practised by the weak on the
strong; indeed, it may be the only way the weak can
escape the domination of the strong. When the
physical aggressor has his mind messed with by the
wily innocent – say, a kidnap victim – this qualifies
as a case of mindfucking; it is the physically weak
using her only resource of power – psychological
power – to withstand the aggressor (and as such we
do not condemn it). But it is, nevertheless, always a
case of psychological domination and manipulation,
unwelcome to the recipient (if only they knew what
was going on). The notions of lying and bullshitting
do not have such a strong connotation of the abuse
of power, although they do visit unwelcome effects
on their victims (namely, false beliefs). The mindfuck,
by contrast, is essentially a kind of victimization,

causing real psychological harm. The harm is not incidental to it, a mere by-product of the intended result; it is integral to what is intended. The agent is mischievous at best and may be homicidal at worst. The simple liar or bullshitter may merely be trying to get out of a tight corner by playing fast and loose with the truth, but the dedicated mindfucker has a wicked will (as old-fashioned moralists would say): he *intends* harm.

It is essential to lying, bullshitting and mind-fucking that the agent misrepresents his true intentions: he gives a false impression of what he is up to. He purports to be telling the truth, and to have the best interests of his listener at heart, but in reality he does not. In doing so, he relies on the *trust* placed in him by the victim. We trust the speaker to be truthful and well intentioned, and he gives us every sign that he is, but he betrays that trust. This, too, is part of the very nature of this family of verbal misdeeds: they involve a breach of trust. The same is not true of, say, verbal bullying or harassment; there is no deceptive abuse of trust in these cases. But the deceptive character of our unholy triumvirate of abuses of language (and other communication systems) brings in the issue of breaches of trust directly, and this adds an extra dimension to their wrongness. Not only is your mind messed with in the mindfuck, resulting in psychological harm, but your trust in the speaker is betrayed. This can naturally lead to difficulties of trust in the future, as the fear of betrayal persists. Thus the mindfuck has the character of *lasting* harm; it is not over with once the mindfuck has been exposed for what it is. It has reverberations over time. There is a generalized loss of confidence in others. There is a *severity* to the mindfuck (as, again, the strength of the language suggests). For all betrayal is experienced as severe, and extends beyond the act itself.

The would-be mindfucker must obviously gain your trust before he can betray it. He must convince you that he is your friend before he can work his evil magic on you. There must, in other words, be a preliminary period of *seduction*. The most obvious illustration of this involves actual seduction: first seduce the other person in the sexual sense, then mindfuck them into paroxysms of jealousy, with or without true cause. (I came across a vivid story of this kind on the internet, intended to clarify the meaning of "mindfuck".) But an analogue of sexual seduction is necessary in other kinds of case too: it is important to gain intimacy of some sort, to establish a basis of trust, before the mindfuck can get off the ground. A period of seduction is important to the success of the enterprise, for this permits the establishment of trust. The mindfuck accordingly requires some planning and forethought, as well as psychological acuity; not for nothing do people speak of the "art of the mindfuck" (and the science too.)

Before I give some examples to illustrate these points, I want to note a certain kind of complicity that characterizes the successful mindfuck. The mindfuck is unwelcome, certainly, but it also arises from weaknesses in the victim. The perpetrator must pluck the right sensitive strings, but the strings have to exist and resonate for the plucking to get anywhere. The irrational fears that are played on must be susceptible to the perpetrator's machinations. The victim is, in other words, *disposed* to be mindfucked, antecedently set up for it. It is hard to state this point with any precision, but I think it is intuitively evident. A liar does not need to appeal to any weakness on the part of the listener, just a habit of believing what he is told, but a mindfucker trades on the specific vulnerabilities of his victim and this makes the victim complicit in his own victimization.

This is not to *blame* the victim; it is merely to point out that he plays a non-trivial causal role in his own demise. For example, the man who is thrown into fits of groundless jealousy by a mindfuck is made so only because he is already prone to jealousy, which is, so to speak, his own problem. This is not the same as being straightforwardly lied to about the fidelity of his beloved; it is more a matter of arousing a dormant jealous tendency by hints and questions. The mindfucker exploits what is already present in his victim: he smells fertile ground. In a certain sense, then, all mindfucking is, at least in part, self-inflicted. It is a manipulation of the antecedent make-up of the victim, not just the insertion of something from outside (like the simple lie). The victim must be *receptive* to the deceptions and invocations of the perpetrator. Anxieties, phobias and prejudices are what typically lead to such receptivity, and they play their indispensable role in producing the end result.

❧ Some illustrations

I have now assembled the conceptual components of the complex concept *mindfuck*. They comprise: trust, deception, emotion, manipulation, false belief and vulnerability. With these materials in hand, we can now consider some examples of the phenomenon, and attempt a rough taxonomy. To my mind, the classic example of the mindfuck occurs in Shakespeare's *Othello*, with Iago's deception and demolition of the "noble moor". Iago has a reputation for directness and honesty, solid soldier that he is, although he is actually deceptive and devious, demonically so. He puts his sturdy reputation to effective use in persuading Othello that his new wife, Desdemona, is being unfaithful to him with his lieutenant Cassio, producing in Othello intense

and violent jealousy, leading finally to the murder of
Desdemona by her crazed husband. Iago's proce-
dure is insinuation and reluctant admission, not so
much direct lying (although there is some of that);
he plays on Othello's vulnerabilities perfectly, timing
his suggestions with exquisite psychological acuity.
One of his chief tactics is to exploit Othello's sense
of racial difference, suggesting that Desdemona
cannot really love a black man, at least beyond an
initial infatuation at his sheer novelty. He creates
in Othello's susceptible and credulous mind a lurid
fantasy of gross sexual licence on Desdemona's part,
which is totally at odds with the facts. This results
in the complete breakdown of Othello's hitherto
robust personality, along with homicidal urges in
relation to his wife. All the elements of the mindfuck are present: the initial trust; the large-scale
deception, subtly perpetrated; the exploitation of
pre-existing weaknesses in the subject's personality;

the emotional tumult that results. Iago provides hints, from which Othello draws his own (erroneous) conclusions, letting Othello do much of the work of destroying himself. Iago, who is Othello's military subordinate, comes to occupy the position of power in the relationship, as he manipulates Othello's emotions at will, and he relishes this reversal of potency. There is, indeed, something perversely erotic in Iago's relationship with Othello, as if Iago is sexually assaulting his general (which, in a way, he is). He could have plotted simply to kill Othello, but that would not have satisfied his motivating desire, which is to dominate and control Othello's mind, to make Othello's soul his plaything. He creates alarm and confusion in Othello, as well as searing jealousy, and these are the distinguishing marks of the mindfuck. Shakespeare does not, of course, employ the term, or any obvious Elizabethan synonym, but he is certainly exploring the syndrome with his customary psychological perspicacity. We are made witness to how manipulated belief leads to emotion, which generates further belief, and then further emotion, until the subject collapses under the weight of delusion and turmoil (as Othello literally collapses at the height of Iago's assault on his being). And Shakespeare leaves us in no doubt about Iago's evil in perpetrating his merciless mindfuck; it might even be suggested that Shakespeare chose it as his supreme emblem of evil. Feigning concern for another, while all the while plotting their downfall, is the height of dastardliness.

This kind of example illustrates the personal, local mindfuck, but there is also the collective, institutional mindfuck. We already have established terms that denote allied phenomena: "indoctrination", "brainwashing", "propaganda". A government or religious sect can engage in methods that approximate the mindfuck: they instil a set of beliefs,

generally false, sometimes wildly so, along with
accompanying emotions, by methods other than
rational persuasion: typically, by appealing to fear
and anxiety. The medieval conception of hell must
qualify as a perfect example: fear of what will
happen after death was used to coerce and control
people according to church dictates, and an elaborate system was devoted to sustaining the illusion.
Fascism and Soviet communism provide obvious
examples too: both appealed to latent prejudices,
resentments and anxieties to manipulate people's
minds (so the population was highly complicit in the
mindfuck practised on them so successfully), and
all the resources of propaganda were brought to
bear. In today's world radical Islam and the communism of North Korea would be plausible candidates
for the honour of being designated by our term
of interest (although we must not exempt our own
political culture from censure). Systematic deception,

yoked to emotions of fear and hatred, is the stamp
of the collective mindfuck, and political systems
that work that way are not difficult to enumerate,
although people will differ, depending on their ideo-
logical preferences, as to how to describe a particular
case. (To what extent was the 2003 Iraq War sold
under false pretences by political propaganda?)
Remember, the mindfuck can never advertise
itself as such, it must always disguise itself as well-
meaning rational persuasion and those in the grip of
it will not recognize their true condition. We outsid-
ers can tell, at least sometimes, but from the inside
it all seems like simple sanity (George Orwell's *1984*
explored this theme trenchantly). Once a person
begins to suspect they have been mindfucked,
however, the power is lost, because the deception
inherent in it has been exposed. The collective mindfuck requires informational isolation, so that nothing
can come along to refute the system of false belief

foisted on its victims; this is why nations and sects that depend on it are always closed societies. The essence of an open society is the free flow of information. The political mindfuck withers under the glare of informational openness, because knowledge thwarts manipulation. But collective mindfucks can be sustained for decades, even centuries, if information is restricted, although they are inherently fragile in the face of the actual facts (hence their ferocity). What is perhaps surprising is how well entrenched and persistent they can become, given their inherent absurdity: once in place they can be tough to dislodge. When people have been mindfucked their whole lives, day in and day out, they find it hard to live in any other way. Their entire psychic configuration becomes geared to the mindfuck. It is as if they become addicted to it. Indeed, human history can sometimes look like a huge series of cults and creeds, superstitions and dogmas, prejudices and

phobias, all held in place by the power of the collective mindfuck. The human psyche seems especially
prone to this kind of quasi-sexual ravishment.

A related type of example is known in military
circles as "PSYOPS": psychological operations. The
purpose of PSYOPS is to undermine the morale of
the enemy or to win the support of an alien population. It does not take the form of presenting a
logically argued case that any rational person can
evaluate; it uses whatever psychological methods
are effective in wearing down, or bringing round,
its target population. These may well include calcu-
lated offences to the deeply held convictions, usually
religious, of the population in question, as well
as promises of a brighter future, whether these
promises can be fulfilled or not. This is the employment of the mindfuck as a weapon of war (hence
the phrase "psychological warfare"), not a matter
of securing rational belief by appeals to the truth

(although if that does the job, well and good); it is matter of producing a particular psychological effect – often, undermining morale. Deception is permitted, even encouraged, so long as it produces compliance. Interrogators use similar techniques to "break people down", to "screw with their heads": they exploit perceived weaknesses in order to render the subject psychologically pliable. This all comes under the heading of institutional mindfucking, as I am construing the term. Part of the utility of the concept is that it brings together these diverse phenomena, so that we can see what is common to them, and what their essential structure is. And we can also evaluate them from an ethical point of view.

There is another category of mindfuck that is quite distinct from those mentioned so far: works of art, particularly films. In certain films the protagonist is in the dark about the true situation in which he finds himself (he may be the subject of a mindfuck), *and so is the audience.* We think we know what is going on, but then late in the day we are shown to have been as massively in error as the protagonist: we have been mindfucked by the film. Examples would be: *Fight Club*, *Sixth Sense*, *The Usual Suspects*, *Mulholland Drive* and *The Crying Game*. In watching each of these films we make certain natural assumptions, encouraged by what we see and hear, but these assumptions turn out to be totally mistaken: we have been tricked, bamboozled. The effect is both pleasurable and annoying: we feel misled and mistreated by the film, perhaps blaming ourselves for excessive credulity, but we also enjoy the feeling of having been led down the garden path. If we had been mindfucked like this in real life, the result would have been disagreeable; but in the safety of the cinema we can distance ourselves from such negative emotions. We were misled, true, but only in the service of being entertained, and we learned something about credulity and stock response. There is exhilaration to this, as you come to recognize the flawed belief system that has been craftily installed in your head; you can almost hear it collapsing in a heap around you. This is the negative mindfuck rendered innocuous through fiction. For it to work we have to feel somehow complicit in our deception: the truth was available – the film did not actively lie to us – but we failed to pick up on it. After all, you *might* fall in love with what appears to be a woman only to discover at the crucial moment that she is really a man, as notoriously happens in *The Crying Game*, when a pendulous penis is shockingly revealed beneath the female outfit. That would be the ultimate mindfuck in real life: the *oh-my-god* moment. In the cinema we can experience such a mindfuck without having to be an actual party to it. We have been mindfucked all right, but no real harm has come to us; we even got a kick out of it (future work: *The Joy of Mindfucking*).

The point of citing these examples is to show the concept of mindfucking in action. It has taxonomic power: it unifies disparate phenomena under a common heading, bringing out implicit similarities. The concept has application to politics, personal relationships, religion and films, and no doubt much more. The concept of bullshit has a comparable range and specificity, which is why it too earns its place in our conceptual scheme. Such a concept deserves our articulate understanding.

❦ Extending the concept

W hat I have to say in this section will be much more controversial and speculative than what I have said so far. My aim is to determine whether the concept of mindfucking can shed light on a range of distinct subjects: does it provide a useful and illuminating way to conceptualize certain figures, movements and disciplines? Here I shall perforce be brief and dogmatic, because the range is large and inherently disputable. Still, it seems to me of interest to enquire how far the concept may be extended.

Frankfurt wonders whether there is more bull-shit in the world now than in earlier times, and he links this question to the pervasiveness and power of the media. He suggests that people feel the need to pretend to a competence they do not really possess, and this leads them to bullshit often. There is simply more *pressure* to bullshit. That may well be so, but my question is different (although related): is there more mindfucking now than ever before? I think the answer is complex. On the one hand, the rise of the media, particularly the internet and television, enlarges the scope of potential mindfucking considerably: we just have more stuff coming at us, and it is less and less regulated by agreed standards of rational cogency. A collective mindfuck is easier to perpetrate if there are that many channels available to promote it (and simple repetition is a powerful force). I shall refrain from singling out specific examples from recent history, but I am sure you have your own personal favourites. Surely our buttons are being pushed all the time, and the truth is not always the prime value that guides public discourse (surprise, surprise). We are all, I suspect, more or less comprehensively mindfucked, from womb to tomb (part of my point here is to arm us against this tendency). I certainly feel the pressure constantly – from advertisers, politicians and advocates of one stripe or another – and am conscious of the need to resist it. However, as the mindfucking din increases, through the proliferation and efficiency of the media, so that very multiplicity works against it, for it can always be counteracted by alternative sources of information. The effective mindfuck thrives on unity of message, the absence of a dissenting voice, and this state of affairs will not obtain if the means of communication are free and open (which is why informational monopoly is such a lamentable condition). The most mindfucked societies on the planet are, not accidentally, those with the weakest independent media. So, while we are subject to a great many influences that are out to mindfuck us, we also have access to other sources of information that work against those influences; if nothing else, we have one mindfuck at odds with another (think of two sets of advertisements trying to sell different cars). The same may be true of bullshit: there might be more of it now, as a matter of sheer quantity, but its effect may be less pernicious, because of the plethora of competing voices. The problem is sorting the bullshit and the mindfucking from the honest discourse (and there is no simple litmus test). A serious worry is that people might come cynically to suspect that there is no genuine distinction here (this essay is dedicated to the proposition that there is). At any rate, the question of whether the world is going to hell in a hand basket of bullshit and mindfucking is not settled in the affirmative simply by observing that there are *more* of these things in the world today than previously, since there might well be countervailing forces. My own belief is that mindfucking is on the increase in those sectors of society that decline to be receptive to alternative messages, those that remain informationally encapsulated. It is when it is regarded as sinful or disloyal to listen to certain sources of information that the level of mindfucking increases. Of course, that has always been true of cults that survive by indoctrination and censorship, but the more difficult it becomes to exclude outside voices, the more aggressive the mindfucking needs to become to counteract the free flow of information. Thus we may predict that religious fanaticism, for example, will be most extreme in a society that feels itself under threat from the freedom of information. The manipulation of minds needs to be at its most intense when those minds might, if left to their own devices, form dissenting opinions. Indoctrination will increase the volume if there are whispers from abroad filtering through. After all, there is no need for propaganda if there exists no countervailing source of opinion.

A question that particularly interests me is
whether philosophy, as an intellectual discipline, is
inherently a type of mindfuck. I do not, I hasten
to add, mean mindfuck in the negative sense; I
mean the positive sense that I explained earlier in
connection with paradigm shifts and other fundamental upheavals of thought. And I suspect that it
is, principally because it deals with large and core
questions. Take philosophical scepticism. When you
are first presented with sceptical arguments that set
out to undermine all of your ordinary beliefs about
the world you feel pretty mindfucked; you feel that
fundamental assumptions you have made all your life
have been shown to be defective. You thought you
knew you were surrounded by physical objects and
by other people with minds, but the sceptic comes
along and convinces you that you have no right to
these assumptions. Maybe you are just dreaming or a
brain lolling in a vat, or are stuck in the Matrix, and

maybe those other "people" are merely automata with no consciousness inside. The sceptic shakes you to your epistemological foundations (Hume argues that there is no reason *at all* to believe that the next piece of bread you eat will nourish you!). This feels exhilarating, although disturbing, and you begin to question everything you have taken for granted. How amazing that you cannot even prove you have a body! The world shrinks to your individual momentary consciousness, the solitary Cartesian ego. You feel restructured at the core by such arguments. Was Socrates, great man as he was, not actually one of the supreme mindfuckers of all time (in the positive sense, of course)? He went around the marketplace questioning people's ordinary beliefs about things, showing them that they were really ignorant of even their most basic concepts: he radically undermined their confidence, their sense of intellectual security (and rightly so). After a couple of hours of Socrates' probing interrogation (note the language), *anyone* would feel mindfucked: they would emerge in a daze of doubt and confusion and mental soreness. Much the same might be said of Hume and Berkeley, who both sought to undermine our common-sense beliefs about the world; again, there is a sense that one's habitual worldview has been systematically dismantled and a new one put in its place (Kant, too, has this disorienting effect, what with those transcendent noumena). These philosophers do indeed mess with your head; they disturb and alarm – yet they also thrill. Maybe a large part of the appeal of philosophy is this kind of benign mindfucking: the intellectual ravishing it produces. Philosophy deals in grand revelations, deep upheavals, and this is apt to leave the mind feeling thoroughly shaken up and bruised about.

Here I cannot resist mentioning Wittgenstein (he also comes up in Frankfurt's exploration of bullshit

– he was hyperbolically against it). Wittgenstein believed that ordinary language casts a spell over our minds, deluding and hoodwinking us into making serious philosophical blunders; the only cure was the kind of therapeutic philosophy he practised. The forms of ordinary language deceive us, and they instil in us various philosophical superstitions, to which we obstinately cling (despite their absurdity). For example, we are misled by the similar grammar of words for the mind and for physical objects into supposing that the mind itself is a kind of quasi-spatial object (we speak of having a thought "in mind" as we speak of a marble being *in* a drawer). What is this Wittgensteinian thesis, if not the claim that ordinary language is itself a kind of mindfuck? Ordinary language is a deceptive manipulator of the philosophical mind, Wittgenstein insists, producing perturbations of the intellect. We are victimized by our own words, by our grammar. "Philosophy is a battle against the bewitchment of our intelligence by means of language",[*] he famously asserts, and this might well be paraphrased by replacing "bewitchment" by "mindfucking". In other words, for Wittgenstein, language insidiously and insistently casts a pall of illusion over our intelligence, which we are powerless to resist, and which we find deeply disquieting. Wittgenstein then sees his job as that of reversing the mindfuck practised on us by language, which he describes as a kind of therapy (and are all therapists not concerned with undoing the effects of mindfucks of one kind or another?).

Is love – romantic love – a species of mindfuck? There is plenty of precedent for regarding it as a psychological disturbance, akin to madness. Its capacity to generate delusion is notorious (well explored by Shakespeare in *A Midsummer Night's*

---

[*] Ludwig Wittgenstein, *Philosophical Investigations* (Oxford: Blackwell, 1953), §109.

Dream). It is certainly mind altering, even soul shattering. So we might, not unreasonably, regard the process of falling in love as a mindfuck, willingly undertaken (although hardly voluntary in most cases). It involves an emotional perturbation, and a certain gushing of positive belief. Mindfucks in general often approximate to insanity, and romantic love is of that ilk. If so, Othello was actually mindfucked by Desdemona first, leaving him in a condition of mild (and relatively benign) insanity, and then Iago came along to mindfuck him another way, bringing about another type of insanity. Love, man, it messes with your head. It is a platitude that the smitten individual is very prone to jealousy, so that they can be easily mindfucked in that state. Jealousy and delusion go hand in hand. No one would maintain that love is based on rational persuasion, and the buttons that the beloved pushes may be invisible to anyone but the victim (and then, sometimes, not even to them). Indeed, it is sometimes recognized to be a kind of affect-driven hallucination, as when the erstwhile lover ruefully reports that the scales have fallen from her eyes, and thereupon regains her normal equilibrium. She was under a kind of sensory and cognitive illusion, and her emotions were disturbingly engaged, but now she sees her earlier state for what it was. This accounts for the ambivalence often expressed about the state of being in love: at one moment it can seem like the most valuable thing in the world, a total revelation; at others as mere folly, an exercise in fatuity. To be infatuated is, literally, to be made silly (the fatuity of the infatuated), and this is one symptom of the successful mindfuck. It is as if evolution programmed you to be susceptible to the romantic mindfuck first, before engaging in the regular kind. The victim of state propaganda, note, is often encouraged to *love* the totalitarian leader: to fall under his romantic spell.

Can the mind mindfuck itself? Is there reflexive mindfucking? I noted earlier the complicity of
the mind in its own propensity to be messed with,
but can the causation be more thoroughly internal?
Can the agency of the act come *entirely* from within
the object of the act? Freud certainly thought so,
since in his view the unconscious mind can be the
source of much delusion and mental disturbance.
The unconscious mind in effect mindfucks the
conscious mind, leading to neurosis and much else.
Your conscious life is controlled and manipulated,
according to Freud, by your repressed unconscious
fears and desires, and this control manifests itself in
erroneous beliefs and disturbed affect. Dreams are a
magnificent example of the phenomenon: although
utterly delusory, they impress themselves on their
subject as real occurrences, and they result in
emotions of many kinds. We awake every morning
from a long night of mindfucking by our internal

dream apparatus; nothing messes with the mind more than dreams. The dream does not exactly tell us lies, still less indulge in bullshit, but it certainly misleads us into a state of mind far removed from reality and often steeped in negative affect. (Then, too, there are those revelatory dreams, where suddenly everything becomes clear.) If dreams emanate from the repressed unconscious, as Freud postulated, then it is part of our own mind that messes with us at night. But even if this is the wrong account of how dreams originate, it is still the mind itself that is doing the messing (along with those outside influences that affect its content). So, yes, the mind can mindfuck itself, and does so repeatedly, methodically and mercilessly. Also, whenever we give in to our fears and anxieties, or our rooted prejudices – whenever we let ourselves be carried away by these things – we are in effect mindfucking ourselves. To firmly believe the things that one's psychological

weaknesses suggest and commend, irrespective
of any rational grounds, is a case of reflexive
mindfucking, and clearly not something to be proud
of. Wishful thinking, in other words, is a type of self-
directed mindfuck. Perhaps, indeed, it is true to say
that we can only be mindfucked by someone else if
we already have a tendency to mindfuck ourselves:
to believe our own bullshit, I am tempted to say.
Mindfucking begins at home. "Go fuck yourself",
people derisively say: difficult physically, to be sure,
but mentally not too much of a feat.

Chemicals in the brain can also produce a potent
mindfuck; in fact, the term was coined partly to
describe the effects of drugs. LSD, for instance, can
lead to delusions and negative affect; it can even
lead to disastrous actions. A "bad trip" is a negative
mindfuck caused by drugs. If drugs lead to para-
noid suspicions, say, they are effectively mindfuckers:
they mess with your head in the same way a human

agent can. (Perhaps some drugs should be officially labelled "MF".) The same may be said of the kinds of "natural" chemicals that produce mental illnesses, such as schizophrenia. The schizophrenic is also mindfucked by chemicals (perhaps originally by his genes): his beliefs and attitudes are cut off from reality, his emotions disturbed. So your brain, as an electrochemical system, can mindfuck you, as well as your mind. Chemicals in the brain can produce the same sorts of psychological effects as the intentional actions of people: seriously erroneous beliefs and disturbed affect, with spiralling interactions between them. We can readily imagine Othello suffering an onset of mental illness, without any outside prompting, which left him with the same symptoms as Iago's deliberate actions. Perhaps one of the worst things about a severe mindfuck caused by another agent is that it simulates mental illness only too closely; and people who have been badly mindfucked do speak as if they have endured a bout of insanity. Certainly, the combination of delusion and affective disturbance is characteristic of insanity. The really potent intentional mindfuck could even be the cause of genuine insanity, as with exceptionally systematic and intense brainwashing. Insanity is, as it were, what the mindfuck aspires to produce, and what we must struggle to avoid.

ॐ Conclusion

Frankfurt, in writing an essay on bullshit, had to face the question of whether what he had written was itself bullshit, the academic kind. (It was not.) I have written an essay on mindfucking, and the question will arise as to whether this essay is itself an exercise in mindfucking (although an exceptionally pedantic one). I do not think, however, that it could possibly be taken that way, because I have not sought to impart any radically new beliefs to my reader; I have simply tried to articulate what is implicit in our ordinary concepts (which is what analytic philosophers are supposed to do). Nor have I, I trust, caused any alarm or confusion in my reader, any mental disequilibrium (although maybe some linguistic discomfort). I do not think there are any great surprises in what I have tried to impart here: no paradigm shifts are on offer. I have simply tried to bring order and clarity to a neglected sector of our language, and show how reality is structured by that sector.

Have I been serious or is this all just an elaborate joke? Yes, I have been serious, although it is hard to resist some of the verbal humour that comes with a topic so named. So, no, I insist, this is *not* a mindfuck: it is an essay *on* mindfucking. It is a treatise on one aspect of human nature, an aspect fraught with personal and political meaning. It will have served its purpose if it alerts the reader to a phenomenon on which it is advisable to have a clear grip.

ॐ About the author

Colin McGinn is Professor of Philosophy at the University of Miami. He was formerly Professor of Philosophy at Rutgers and Wilde Reader in Mental Philosophy at Oxford. He is the author of over a dozen works of philosophy and his autobiographical *The Making of a Philosopher* (2002) is an acclaimed bestseller.